Recalculating

Gail Mosley

Published by Otley Word Feast Press 2015
OWF Press Community Interest Company
9B Westgate, Otley, West Yorkshire, LS21 3AT

ISBN 978-0-9927616-6-0

CONTENTS

Nightingale 1

Recalculating 2

Lamb White Days 3

Bicycle 4

Mum's Sewing Machine 5

Skaters.. 6

When I was ill 7

Times of Buses 8

My Dog Wilf 9

Cousin Jerry... 10

Like Pirates 11

Mental Health 12

Deer... 13

Outing 14

That Time 15

Red Cyclamen... 16

Request 17

Friends in the Northwest 18

Fallers... 19

There Will be Two Hymns 20

Prodigal 21

Love All... 22

Deuce 23

Game Set Match.. 24

Nightingale

If ever I'm blown apart
bleeding
doing my best to live
despite the odds,
don't give me a song
from that damned square,
give me the roar
of the nightingale.
Give me one who's tough;
trained to tend the filth
and gore with down
to earth procedures,
hold things together,
get things done,
rest, recoup,
– whatever way is best;
bed, bar, marathon
adventure –
return, repeat
the worn routine,
the shock refrain,
vocation.

Recalculating

Some days we spread our arms like wings
to catch an updraft of reprieve.
The diagnosis throws us into free-fall.
We tuck in elbows, bend at the knee
in hope of easy landing,
but all in all we know the end;
our span is finite
as it never seemed before.
We note the jewel-light,
the slow sure spin,
feel a freedom that mimics flight.

Lamb White Days

Can we go down to the river?
Walk down the speckled ribbon road
pegged with singing telegraph poles,
past those two horses in their field,
over the worn stone stile where nettles
wait, down sheltered primrose banks
into the path of the river's breeze.
Tea-brown water gossips and spits
around tablecloth stones, gulps pebbles
we throw, swallows them whole

– can we go down to the river,
watch how it seethes and races
high white clouds into the blue,
under the bridge, for ever?

Bicycle

Raleigh from the 60s
893 parts

scrabble for left pedal
push and away
surprise of hard saddle
soon forgotten

whip of wind waver
handlebar steer
insect-leg frame leans
into the bend

ground-touch fleeting
through whisper
of rubber

whisk of spokes
rolling and bowling and flying

893 parts plus one

Mum's Sewing Machine

Not a Singer but the next best thing – a Jones.
My mother heard a rumour, queued for you
one long cold day in Nottingham, heaved
your dead weight onto the bus
that Grandma met, balanced you on my pram.
They say I squalled the whole way home.

Your black curves and gold scrolled lettering,
your clackety shuttle busy for years turning collars,
stitching remnants, transforming bargain lengths
into blouses, skirts and dresses,
letting down, turning up, taking in,
saving sheets sides-to-middles.
You sit in the corner now, forgotten,
a Jones – never quite a Singer.

Skaters

Three of us in a line, schoolgirl faces
startled into smiles.
Two in giggle-wobbly hired boots
clinging to the cousin in the middle
– pristine skates, plaid skirt –
sixty years ago in black and white.

At family gatherings we laugh, *let's do
the photograph. How did we stand?*
We form up close, smile,
a half-remembered moment
still on ice.

When I was ill
(After CK Williams' My Mother's Lips)

She knew everything – when I was tired, or lying; she'd know
I was ill before I did

and let me sleep through breakfast-time, coming in with a tray
and a bottle of medicine

saying, you're not going to school today, take a spoonful
of this and try a few cornflakes,

as my head grew aware of its' throbbing and shivers took
over my shoulders

and a chill from the sheets enveloped my body, so she switched
on the fire that was never switched on

except when I was ill which was maybe twice a year and always
lasted about three weeks

so that a rumour trickled back to us that the school would be
sending an Attendance Officer

although one never appeared, and I don't know whether my mother
sent a note or word of mouth

as we didn't have a phone and if she called the doctor,
which she rarely did, she'd walk up to the corner,

to the phone-box on the main road, with four pence in her pocket.

Times of Buses

When fairies rode the roofs of buses
down to Plymouth Hoe
and grassy castles could be captured
with a flag and boys played two-ball
in the avenue 'til dark,
buses, parks and avenues breathed time.

Today at dusk a golden room rolls past
half empty, fitted to mortal needs,
but for a moment, wondrous.
Time takes a breath, moves on;
next stop the park, the avenue.

My Dog Wilf

Wilf's a wolfhound, bony, bristled,
comes at once when he's whistled,
bounds down beaches flip-flop-pawed,
tugs my conscience if ignored.

I'll shout his name from now 'til never,
ours is a bond that none can sever.
I dreamed him up one cold wet January;
Wilf's my dog, and he's imaginary.

Cousin Jerry

Riding high on the Ordinary, joke top-hat,
patchwork jacket, carnival man

lived next door when we were little,
created things from wood and metal;

sculptures, models, gadgets, engines,
go-karts, toys, automatons.

Rode with mates in bikers' leather.
Married Bernie, jewellery maker.

Fitted kitchens, an actor's boat,
hand-made cabinets, all bespoke.

A whizz with clocks in Switzerland
until the time that time ran down.

Asked for a party, fancy dress,
Led Zeppelin, a side-car hearse.

Still I see the Penny Farthing,
top-hat tipped, broad face smiling,

listen for the last laugh laughing.

Like Pirates

Hammer of keys locks the front room down,
uneven bursts of tapping, line-end pings
followed by the growl of Return.
Shush, he's working, she whispers,
not daring to disturb the pipe-smoke air
too soon before dinner.
Routine is what he sets his watch by

and she runs the house like clockwork,
cleans and polishes to a shine
he dare not fingerprint or breathe on.
Like a game of pirates in the gym,
balance is everything, any wobble
or skirmish righted in a grumbling return,
each to their own safe ground.

Mental Health

One psychiatrist down, no replacement soon.
The system unravels faster than my father's mind;
a ragged hole, no care, no safety net,
no last resort prescription.

My father, lost,
something is happening
I don't think I'm going mad
I don't want that

What can we do when interloping dogs
invade his bed but let them lie; try to recognise
the reframed weave of threads?
One psychiatrist down; a gap too wide.

Deer

The day he died I stood at the window
in a strange room.
He's died, I said.
He's died.

Dark came down on the Shropshire hills,
and the moon was there,
and below my window on the ashy grass
a small deer stood for a second or two.

Yes, a deer,
I said.

Outing

I'd like to go to Driffield, it must be over a year...
Fish and chips at the restaurant, the waitresses
remember her. Then across to Brown's,

easing through the amber den stuffed
with calf-hide, waxed cotton, tweed: up half a floor
 to brighter chiffon, silks, straw hats,

but in the fag-end of a sale find no bargains
save a stripy top in red and white.
We take our leave

with steady nerve past stands of shooting-sticks
and black umbrellas, gain the High Street.
There's more choice in Beverley, she says.

Driving home we call in at the Farm Shop
for cheese and ground-rice tarts. Another
place they used to go.

That Time

My aunt retells how they travelled
up The Great North Road to visit.
How grand it was; the country air,
the village, the cottage,
the walk past two horses, their field,
and down to the bridge, the river,
those big flat rocks.

How my father would hoist me
shoulder-high and step
across the stones while they worried
on the bank; *he'll fall, he'll drop her,*
which of us will go in after ...

He didn't falter and I held on tight.

He always got there, not like me,
she shifts in her chair. *I never thought*
he'd be the first to go.

Red Cyclamen

Last of the unexceptional gifts,
a bit of a jostle and flounce,
we break up the row of cacti,
brighten the window-sill.

If we were bees we'd dance for her.
If we were birds we'd sing.
If we were fish we'd shoal around her.

But we are raggedy flags,
fingers up to the gloom outside,
the nearest there'll be to raging,
here, tonight.

Request

Take me to the flat lands
where space and form and colour
are enough,

to a house, to a room with a plain
wooden table and chair, bread,
cheese, fruit in a bowl, a thin-handled
frying pan and a toasting fork,

where no-one will ever be pleased,
so there's no need to try.

Friends in the Northwest

First their shapes, large outlines
becoming in this season's white.
Then faces, creased, shaved, unchanged.
Lastly, names. I can't help
saying the names.

It isn't odd that they have names;
these that will still be old
when our names are gone.
We like to say they call us
but that's not it, listen,
Haystacks, Scafell, Skiddaw,
Helvellyn, Coniston Old Man.

Fallers

They're turning turtle, the old ones.
Everywhere you see them
full length on dodgy pavements,
propped bleeding against walls,
circled by kneeling helpers
while the ambulance is called.

Today I'm one of them, abruptly
floored outside the joke shop.
Helping hands reach down.
Are you alright? Yes, I'm alright.

Bruised palms: alright. Banged knee:
alright. Glasses' frame: bent.
Split self: one of me walking on,
distanced from the self who sprawled
in that ostentatious way.

There Will be Two Hymns

First, *The Old Rugged Cross.*
No one knows the tune or how the words fit.
No one believes except perhaps her mother,
head bowed, in the front pew.
We cannot sing and yet we try our best.
Its awfulness takes the edge off loss.

Second, *All Things Bright and Beautiful.*
We all know the tune, how well the words fit,
that it belongs to the living, to the two boys
in clean white shirts at attention in the front pew.
We cannot sing and yet we try our best.
It's what we have come for, all we can do.

Prodigal

Sure, he says, sure,
and we are, for a moment,
reassured, seeing him,
as we'd like him to be.

Sure, we say, sure,
but the moment slips by
and we know, after all,
that we have to allow him
licence. Let him be.

Love All

We played at two-ball in the avenue
with perfect throw and catch, a wordless game.
I didn't need to shout or call to you,
I can't remember if I knew your name
but you were tall and willowy and fair,
and we could play for ever and a day,
at least until dusk blurred the evening air,
and each of us was called our separate way.

The accidental grace we conjured then,
oblivious to ordinary fears,
I've tried to capture many times again,
and keep returning to it down the years.

I wonder if it meant as much to you
when we played two-ball in the avenue.

Deuce

You are a sod in all you say and do
at home, at work, with mates, on holiday,
so why on earth am I still here with you?
Beyond belief is what my friends all say.

I hate the way you slurp your rum and black
as nightcap when you've staggered from the pub
and turn on us with jeering mouth gone slack,
hands groping for a misplaced roll-up stub.

Get out, just go, I want to scream and shout,
but that, of course, would make things even worse.
I stop my tongue, resolve to wait it out.
No point in wasting breath on rant or curse.

Decision made tonight will be for good.
I'm set to make the move I know I should.

Game Set Match

They're playing tennis
the other side of the hedge,

heads, shoulders, arms, racquets,
appearing and dropping out of sight

and the ball curving over and back,
cutting the air, each arc

solid as a lemon slice,
delicious frisson bite

to savour later
in an empty garden.